Rebecca Manley Pippert

know

Your life with Christ

LIVE | GROW | **KNOW**

thegoodbook
COMPANY

Know
© Rebecca Manley Pippert, 2015

Published by
The Good Book Company
Tel (US): 866 244 2165
Tel (UK): 0333 123 0880
International: +44 (0) 208 942 0880
Email: info@thegoodbook.com

Websites:
North America: www.thegoodbook.com
UK: www.thegoodbook.co.uk
Australia: www.thegoodbook.com.au
New Zealand: www.thegoodbook.co.nz

Unless indicated, all Scripture references are taken from the HOLY BIBLE,
NEW INTERNATIONAL VERSION. Copyright © 1979, 1984, 2011 by Biblica. Used by permission.

ISBN: 9781910307670

All rights reserved. Except as may be permitted by the Copyright Act, no part of this publication
may be reproduced in any form or by any means without prior permission from the publisher.

Published in association with the literary agency of Wolgemuth and Associates, Inc.

Printed in the Czech Republic
Design by André Parker

Contents

Introduction 5

How To Use This Handbook 7

1. The Beginning. 9

2. How Life Was Meant To Be 19

3. The Mess We Made Of Things. 29

4. Christ The Lord Of All 41

5. Christ's Return 51

Useful Resources 61

Introduction

When I was a young agnostic searching for answers, I had a conversation with a well-meaning Christian. After some discussion she finally said in exasperation: "Becky, faith is an experience of the heart! Don't let your mind get in the way!" I responded: "But if there is a God and he created us with minds, then why doesn't he want us to use them? Shouldn't true faith offer real answers that help us make sense of life?"

As I continued my spiritual journey (one that eventually led to my becoming a Christian), I discovered that the God of the Bible does want us to know what is true—and that this truth is wonderful.

Christianity is a religion of revelation. God has revealed who he is, who we are, and the purpose and meaning of life, in his word, the Bible. So in KNOW, we will explore the central beliefs of the Christian faith and how they make sense of our world and our lives. We will start before the beginning of human history, and travel right through to beyond the end of history.

In all this, we will be discovering the key truths about God, the world, and ourselves. In other words, we will be studying doctrine—truth. Why does doctrine matter? Because most of life is ultimately a "God problem." Think of the problems we face at various stages of our lives: How do we cope with suffering? How do we find a secure identity in a confusing and ever-changing world? What do we do when we fail, or those we trusted betray us? Where do we find hope that is lasting and true?

The answer lies in knowing the character of God, not in a fingers-crossed human act of wishful thinking. To know who God is enables us to live our lives with confidence, strength and joy. We are able to live our lives with purpose, grit and glory as we live knowing God. Knowing God's truth isn't dry or boring—it is thrilling. I'm so pleased you're joining me as we discover together more of our God, and more of ourselves.

Becky

How To Use This Handbook

Everything you'll need (apart from a Bible and a pen) is in this handbook. Each session has several different elements:

 Introduction. Helps you begin to think about the main theme of the session. You can read in the handbook, or watch Becky on the DVD or download.

 Historical Context. Explains what is going on in the part of the Bible you're about to look at.

 Bible Study. This will take most of your time, as you look at the Bible together and share what you discover as you answer the questions in this handbook. A good Bible translation to use is the "NIV2011." There is space in the handbook to make notes, but it's not compulsory!

 Live What You Learn. The Bible changes us in how we think and act. This section encourages you to think about what difference the section of the Bible you've been reading might make to you.

 Following Jesus. Listen to Becky talk about the main themes of the session. There is a summary of what she says in your handbook.

 Praying Together. A time to speak to God. Prayers don't have to be long or use complicated words; and feel free to pray silently in your head if you don't feel comfortable praying out loud.

 Going Deeper. Something for you to take home to read and think about between sessions. This is entirely optional. If you have any questions, do ask them at the start of the next session.

Note For Leaders: You'll find a concise Leader's Guide for the course, as well as the downloadable videos, at www.thegoodbook.com/know. You'll need the access code in your DVD case to be able to get onto the page.

I. The Beginning

Genesis 1 v 1 – 2 v 3

The very first words in the very first book of the Bible, called Genesis, say: "In the beginning God created..." Today there are many popular views about God. One view tells us to seek the "god within." God is not outside of us, people who believe this say, but within our psyche; therefore we must trust our hearts to guide us. Another view says that God is one with everything, which is pantheism. According to this view, we ourselves are god because we carry the spark of the divine—but so do trees and rocks and cows.

Christianity says something altogether different, which we'll be discovering throughout this series. But for now we must ask: *how do we find out who God truly is?* The Judeo-Christian faith is based, not primarily on what *we* think about God, but on what God has revealed about himself. Biblical faith is rooted not in our discovery but in his disclosure. Christianity is a religion of revelation. God has revealed himself in many ways, but his primary revelation is through his Son, Jesus, and the Bible.

Genesis is a book of beginnings that gives an account of who God is and who we are. Our first study in Genesis chapter one is the fascinating account of how God formed the universe and the first human beings, who were made in his image. While Genesis raises many questions to consider, it also reveals a breadth of conception, artistry, and spiritual and psychological insight that is simply breathtaking, as we shall soon see!

Historical Context

Though the authorship of Genesis is still debated among scholars, Jewish tradition, and the Bible itself, ascribes the authorship of Genesis and the first five books of the Bible to Moses. The date of Genesis is also debated. Many scholars believe it came to be written down around 1300 BC. But one thing is certain: by then, the material in Genesis was not new. It had been orally transmitted for generations. Oral tradition is more accurate than we might think, because the material was structured for easy memorization and it was regarded as sacred.

Who was Moses? He was a Hebrew baby, rescued in a basket from the River Nile by an Egyptian princess. He was raised in the palace as a prince and received the finest education available in his day. But as an adult he left all the luxuries of royal life to accept God's call to liberate his own people from Egyptian slavery and take them to the promised land. Moses led a people who had lived in a world where those around them believed in many, competing gods. Genesis told them how to start looking at life from God's perspective.

How does this ancient document relate to us today? The Israelites needed to know the answers to the big questions of life—and so do we! Who is God? What is my relationship to him? How does knowing God affect the way that I live? Genesis provides exciting answers to life's greatest questions!

 Bible Study

Read Genesis 1 v 1 – 2 v 3

The Israelites had been exposed to the pagan myths of Egypt. They had heard how these many Egyptian deities constantly quarrelled; how the birth of the universe coincided with the gods' battles and their love affairs. These gods were not free and distinct from the world; they didn't stand outside of the world. So the first verse of the Bible would have been a jaw-dropper, because it stood in stark contrast to everything they had heard about pagan deities, and broke all the mythologies of the ancient East.

1. Whether you were a Hebrew who had lived all your life in a neighboring pagan country, or had never even heard of God before, what would you have learned about God already in verse 1?

_____

_____

o What did God need in order to be able to create the universe, and why is that so significant?

_____

_____

2. What was the earth like in the beginning?

_____

_____

o Genesis shows us that God created the heavens and the earth, but the earth was formless and empty until God brought order, beauty and harmony into being. What does that tell us about God's nature?

_____

_____

As we read the entirety of Scripture, we discover, unsurprisingly, that God's nature is complex. God is described as having a plurality within the unity of his being: he is Father, Son and Holy Spirit. Even as early as Genesis 1 v 1-3, we see hints of the nature of God—that he is one, but there is a distinction within the oneness. God the Father took initiative through speaking his word, but we also see in verse 2 that the Spirit was involved. Later in the New Testament, we learn that Jesus, the Son of God, was the Father's agent in creation: "Through him all things were made; without him nothing was made that has been made" (John 1 v 3). So even as early as Genesis, we have an inkling of the complex nature of God.

3. What does it reveal about God that his commands produce such immediate results?

_____

_____

o What does it reveal about God's nature that he chooses to use words? Why does anyone use words?

_____

_____

_____

4. We see that God issues commands and it is done. But it isn't merely through words that God expresses himself. God is described in verse 2 as a Spirit who hovers over what he has made.

Think of someone in your natural life who "hovers" over loved ones. What does that image reveal about God?

_____

_____

_____

In just the first three verses we learn that God is eternal, without beginning or end. There has never been a time when God was not. He has absolute authority, and created the earth out of non-being; he needed no help. Not only did God's word accomplish exactly what he wanted to accomplish, but God spoke because he wants to be known. He is a communicative God who desires relationship. The Creator God is also not a raw, impersonal power but a personal God, who hovers over his creation like a nurturing parent: a deity brimming with love, delight and nurturing concern.

Christian opinions differ over how we should interpret Genesis 1. But whether we come to the view that God completed the job of creation in six literal twenty-four-hour days, or over a much longer period, the one thing that is absolutely clear is this: God is the creator of all things.

5. What are the repeated words and phrases that occur six times? What does God's response to what he has created reveal about his nature (v 3-24)?

_____

_____

_____

6. What did the commands of the first three days produce?

_____

_____

7. What were the results and purpose of God's commands of the next three days?

_____

_____

8. The biblical attitude to the material world is very different from that of many philosophies and religions which are concerned only with the spiritual and the soul. Their understanding of salvation involves the soul being released from the body to join the non-material world where God lives. But here we read that God joyfully declares that the material world he has created is "good."

How does this shape the way in which we view the physical realm: our bodies, nature, animals and the earth?

_____

_____

9. How were man and woman different from the rest of creation (1 v 26-27)?

_____

_____

o What do you think it means to be made in God's image?

_____

_____

_____

_____

10. What did God commission the man and the woman to do (v 28-30)?

_____

_____

_____

The implications of God's commands are profound. To "be fruitful and increase in number" means to develop the social world: build families, churches, schools, cities, governments, and laws. The second phrase, "subdue [the earth]," means to harness the natural world: plant crops, design computers, create art, compose music or build bridges. In other words, God commissioned human beings to be his vice-regents—to love, protect and nourish all that he had made.

o How does God's evaluation of his creation change after he has created humans (v 31)?

_____

_____

11. How was the seventh day of creation unique (2 v 1-3)?

_____

_____

o The Jewish practice commanded by God (Exodus 20 v 8-11) of a "Sabbath rest" (resting on the seventh day of every week) was directly linked to God's example here.

Why is this command important in our frantic, work-without-boundaries culture?

_____

_____

In Hebrews 4 v 9-11 we are told that it is possible for us to enter God's rest permanently. The New Testament makes it clear that the practice of "Sabbath rest" also points to the deeper understanding of learning to rest in Christ for our salvation, rather than in our works.

 ## Live What You Learn

Genesis makes it clear that while God created the world, he is still above and beyond all that he has made and distinct from it. God created everything, which means that physical matter is neither evil nor divine—it is simply good because it comes from God. But to worship anything God has made (humans, animals or nature) is considered to be idolatry in the Bible, a very serious offense. Everything God created is intended to lead us to worship God, rather than worship what he created!

o *The Westminster Shorter Catechism says: "What is the chief end of man? To glorify God and enjoy him forever." What have you learned about God that causes you to worship him more fully and to enjoy his presence?*

 ## Following Jesus: The Trinity

o In order for us to know what God is like, God must reveal who he is: and God has done exactly that! He came to us as a person: Jesus of Nazareth.

o At Jesus' baptism (Luke 3 v 21-22) we see the three-fold essence of God: the Father, the Son and the Holy Spirit. Jesus always spoke of God as his Father.

o *What then is the Trinity?* It's not simple! There is one God, who exists eternally in three, distinct, equally divine Persons, who have shared each other's life in perfect love for all eternity.

o *The idea of God being a Trinity is very exciting!* At the center of the universe, God is a divine relationship.

- *Why does this matter so much?* Being made in God's image means we're designed for love relationships. It explains why we're wired for intimacy.

- Each Person in the Godhead (the Trinity) lives in self-giving and other-receiving love. We must reflect this way of divine love: loving people and using things, but never the reverse.

- The Trinity reveals that God is love: and he invites us in!

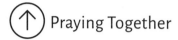 Praying Together

- Take time to praise God for being a God of order, power and creativity. Thank Him for being the Author and King of all creation.

- Thank him for wanting to be personally involved in our lives.

- Ask him to help you to know him better, and to order your lives in accordance with his wisdom so that you may better reflect his image to others.

You'll find some more books about the themes of this session on page 61.

 Going Deeper: Why Work Matters

A much missed and rather surprising aspect of Genesis 1 – 2 is that it shows us that God is a worker—and that we are created to be workers, too.

Our first glimpse of God is God on a working day—six of them, in fact! We see God at work in the creation of the universe in general and our own planet in particular: "We see God the supreme biologist and botanist, the engineer of the Alps and the ant, the architect of galaxies and the designer of butterflies and the first artist, who not only works in color, but invented it!" (Peter Lewis, *The Glory of Christ*). God creates not as some distant force or detached mind, but as a working Person, who marveled and delighted at what he created.

Not only that, but the creatures he made in his image—you and me—were also created to work. At the start, man and woman were given a specific mandate to rule over the creation, to fill the earth and to subdue it, and to enjoy its fruits (1 v 28-30). The work of creation has been finished in its fundamental stages, but human beings are given the "creation project" to develop and manage the earth. We are to take what God has made and shape it and use it for God's good purposes.

There are no negative aspects about work in Genesis 1 and 2, because work is a blessing. As we'll see in Session Three when we reach Genesis 3, work has been spoiled, along with everything else in the world, by the human race's rebellion against God. Now, though work can be fulfilling, it is also often frustrating. Yet work is still one way that we reflect our God-image. God made us to be like him in his creativity and development. We will never build utopia—that will only come about when Christ returns to establish the new earth. But we can work and partner with God to make the world a little bit closer to God's original design. Our work matters.

Our motive for work is to bring God glory in everything we do. How do we glorify God through our work? First, by recognizing that we are not primarily servants of human beings, but of Christ! We live to serve him in all we do—and that makes all the difference. Second, by consciously relying on God's power to help us do our work creatively and well. Third, by striving to do our job with excellence because we worship a God of excellence. That means a secretary's typing should be accurate and sharp, the surgeon's incisions should be clean, and the meals we feed our families are to be nutritious and pleasing—because God is a God of order and beauty and excellence. All work is worthy and worthwhile when it is a response to God's calling, done in God's way, for his glory.

We work to provide for our legitimate needs. The apostle Paul was one of the greatest missionaries who ever lived. He was also a tentmaker by trade and he used his work to cover his own expenses. We were not made for inactivity or unproductiveness. Our capacity and need to work is part of our human dignity and significance. The Bible has strong words for those who are idle—those who can work, but do not: "'The one who is unwilling to work shall not eat.' We hear that some among you are idle and disruptive ... Such people we command and urge in the Lord Jesus Christ to settle down and earn the food they eat" (2 Thessalonians 3 v 10-12). Paul is clear that to refuse to work when one is able and a job is available is sinful.

We work to provide for the needs of others. It is through our vocation that we obey God's call to serve our neighbor and partner with God in loving care for the world. The joy of work is that it enables us to provide for our children when they are young, or relieve the suffering of those who have experienced drought or displacement, or contribute to the beauty or functionality of the surroundings that others live in. The apostle Paul said: "In everything I did, I showed you [the church in Ephesus] that by this kind of hard work we must help the weak, remembering the words the Lord Jesus himself said: 'It is more blessed to give than to receive'" (Acts 20 v 35).

Our work provides opportunity for witness. When we work, we are normally shoulder to shoulder with those who do not know the Lord. We witness through our *being* by revealing the beauty of the character of Christ. That means we do not engage in gossip or office politics and we rejoice when another receives the promotion we wished for. We witness through our *doing* by doing our job with excellence and by demonstrating acts of kindness. "Let your light shine before others, that they may see your good deeds and glorify your Father in heaven" (Matthew 5 v 6). And we witness through *telling*, though usually this is outside our work hours, because our boss doesn't pay us to take time off work to present the gospel. It takes people time to see how we live our lives. But people pay attention. As trust develops and we talk at lunch or invite friends for a coffee or dinner, they will probably be curious about what makes us tick and may have wondered what makes us different.

There will be work in eternity! When the prophets look forward to the renewal of the earth when Christ returns at the end of history, they do not imagine that work ceases. Rather, they speak of building, planting and enjoying the fruits of one's labours (Isaiah 65 v 21-22). When God recreates this world perfectly, it will be a planet of activity and discovery—of work that is always fulfilling, and never frustrating, just as God designed it to be.

Reflection Questions

One thing that enables us to see the importance of our work is when we understand what the Bible has to say about our profession.

o *If you were to describe the nature of your work (or your present focus of study) in just one word, what would it be?*

o *What does the Bible say about your work? For example, for journalists (truth); for doctors (healing); for lawyers (justice); for raising children (wisdom); for helping professions (service).*

o *How does this biblical knowledge help you understand how to glorify Christ through your work? For example, Christians who are artists should not be unremittingly dark (as so much contemporary art is), nor sentimental or saccharine or simply commercial (doing whatever sells).*

2. How Life Was Meant To Be

Genesis 2 v 4-25

Last week we studied Genesis chapter 1 in order to understand who God is and who we are. What did we learn in Genesis 1?

First, *God has no peer or competitor*. He created an ordered universe. The sun and moon are his handiwork—not his rivals, as most believed in the ancient East. His word is supreme: a simple command is sufficient. He speaks and it is done. Yet God is personally involved with his creation. His Spirit was described as hovering over his creation, as a mother or father lovingly hovers over little children.

Second, *God is King and Lawgiver*. He divides and names the light and darkness, and the land from the sea. He appoints the stars for fixed times. He creates humans and tells them to be fruitful and multiply and govern the earth.

Next, *God reveals himself personally*. He wants us to know who he is. He has personal attributes such as love and delight—joy and authority.

Fourth, *the earth reflects its Creator*. Each area reflects God and obeys him: the waters remain separate from earth, and the light from darkness; the sun rules the day, and the moon and stars rule the night. There is order, not chaos, at the center of life.

Finally, *human beings are the apex of his creation*. Everything was made for man's benefit and God's glory! People were made in the image of God. They were created to know God, to reveal God to the rest of his creation, and to rule the world as his stewards, under his sovereign rule. Human beings were made by God, to know God.

Now let's look at a much more focused and delightful account of God creating human beings in Genesis chapter 2.

 ## Historical Context

The first thing we notice is that this is a second account of creation. Unlike chapter 1, chapter 2 doesn't describe the creation of the whole universe. Instead, like a telescope, it focuses intimately on the creation of a garden and of Adam and Eve. That is why there are so many details on the geographical location. In other words, Genesis 2 isn't trying to tell exactly the same story that we read in chapter 1.

We will see that God prepared a beautiful garden in Eden. Biblical scholars believe the garden was probably located in the vicinity of ancient Mesopotamia and modern Iraq. A river originated in the garden, and then split into four branches.

It should also be pointed out that in chapter 1, the Hebrew name *Elohim*, which is used for God, is a more generic term for the most high God. But in chapter 2 the Hebrew word used for God is *Yahweh*, which is God's personal name. Why? Because now God has a personal relationship with human beings!

 ## Bible Study

Read Genesis 2 v 4-17

1. In what ways is the creation of humans unique among the rest of creation (v 7)?

_____

_____

_____

2. What role did Adam play in the process of his own creation? What is the significance of this?

_____

_____

3. What is the significance of God breathing life into Adam, beyond his merely being physically alive?

_____

_____

When God breathed into Adam, he was giving human beings a God-consciousness, enabling them to hear God's voice and respond to him. Man's uniqueness is that only humans are made in the image of God. We are not meaningless pieces of protoplasm, a set of chemicals or a fortuitous arrangement of atoms! We have been given souls, which means we have self-conscious life, including abilities such as reason.

4. Describe the garden that God prepared for Adam (v 8-9).

_____

_____

_____

5. What responsibilities, freedoms and boundaries did God give Adam (1 v 28; 2 v 15-17)?

_____

_____

_____

God gives only one prohibition in the garden—they are not to eat from "the tree of the knowledge of good and evil" (2 v 17) because they have been created as creatures to love and obey their Creator. God gave humans a great deal of freedom (to create, to use our gifts, to build and explore), but we are not given the freedom to "know," or decide, what is good and evil—that is, to be God over the world. The only thing humanity must *not* do is to stop enjoying being created beings, and instead grasp at the status of being Creator.

Don't miss the fact that they were able to access fruits from all other trees—including the tree of life. God's will and intention for them was to live forever.

o Though it's sometimes wrongly assumed that work is punishment, how are we to view work from God's perspective?

_____

_____

_____

Read Genesis 2 v 18-25

6. It is fascinating that even in Eden we hear God say that something "is not good." What do we learn about human nature in Genesis 2 v 18?

_____

_____

_____

When God acknowledges Adam's need for human companionship, he then asks Adam to go through the process of naming all the animals, perhaps to help Adam recognize his loneliness and his need for a human companion.

7. Describe Adam's sudden burst of ecstasy on meeting Eve. What was it that Adam saw in Eve that made him think that she must have come from him? What does it suggest in terms of their relationship?

_____

_____

_____

"Suitable helper" literally means "a help as opposite him"; in other words, one that is suited and complementary (not identical) to him. Adam's response is the first poetry we hear uttered from human lips in the Bible. Eve is to stand at his side, her soul bound to his in harmony and intimacy and love.

8. In the accounts of the creation of Adam and Eve, they are both passive. It is God who initiates and acts. Indeed, God's role in introducing them seems to that of matchmaker! Here is the beginning of God ordaining and creating the institution of marriage.

What is God's three-fold intent in creating the institution of marriage (2 v 24-25)?

_____

_____

_____

Here, in the perfect ease between them, we see God's true pattern and creation design. Note that there is no distrust or dishonour or envy or accusation—but be prepared for what is about to happen in the next chapter!

 ## Live What You Learn

Being created by God meant that Adam and Eve were to live within the limits of their humanity—in loving dependence upon God, the Author of life. Being made finite and dependent meant they had been created to be fulfilled in God. They were to rejoice in their dependence on God and reject any claim to false autonomy. Loving obedience to God was what would ensure their freedom and happiness.

o *What have we learned about who God is, and the kind of life God originally intended for us?*

o *What does this passage teach us about how we find our identity and what it means to be truly human...*

    — in our relationship to God?

    — in our work? And our care for the earth?

    — in our relationships?

Following Jesus: The Living God

- God is not a force or an energy field—he's a living Person! The Bible writers refer to him as "the living God," because he's intimately involved with the people he has made.

- In 2 Kings 18 and 19, King Hezekiah turned to the Lord when Israel was threatened by Sennacherib. He asked God to intervene, and he did.

- We have been created to know God and to relate to him intimately, but also to rule under God's gracious rule. The story of David and King Saul in 1 Samuel shows what happens when a person refuses to surrender to God's rule.

  - An enemy giant—the Philistine Goliath—was terrifying Israel's army with threats of destruction and was mocking their God.

  - King Saul did not turn to God for help, but David was confident that the living God would save his people—so he defeated Goliath.

  - David went on to rule Israel—and unlike Saul, he did so under God's sovereign rule.

- When we feel overwhelmed by life's difficulties, will we trust in appearances or the unseen living God? No matter how things look, God has the last word. He loves us and is truly there.

 ## Praying Together

- Thank God for his love and graciousness in creating us.

- Ask God to help us live in joyful dependence upon him, as we were created to do.

- God made us relational beings because it reflects his own essence. Perhaps pray for any relational difficulties you may be experiencing.

- God created work to be a blessing, not a curse! Ask him to bless the work you are engaged in and to use it to glorify God.

You'll find some more books about the themes of this session on page 61.

Going Deeper: What It Means For You To Be You

The pop singer Madonna once said in an interview: "I try to change my identity every few years. I live to recreate myself." The same article quoted another singer, Lady Gaga, who said: "I change my identity with every new show!"

The concept of identity is a subject of great fascination for modern people. How do we discover who we truly are? Is our identity determined by the "face" we create to wear at work, like Madonna? Or the "face" we wear with our parents or with our friends? And once we work out who we are, we then find ourselves wondering: What is our purpose? Why we are here?

When it comes to our sense of identity and purpose, sociologists have noted a significant change that took place as we moved from the traditional world to the modern world. In the pre-modern world, identity was something that was determined by the family and social status you were born into. Likewise, your profession was handed down to you. Work meant following in the footsteps of parents and grandparents.

The positive aspect of pre-modern life was that there was a great sense of security. Identity and roles were clear. The negative aspect, however, was the lack of freedom. What if your gifts didn't fit the work that your family did?

But our modern world is very different. The chief features of modern life are choice and change. Our identities are not given, but achieved. We create our own identities and we choose our own work. We are not required to follow what our parents did for a living.

The positive aspects of our modern life, of course, are freedom, creativity and choice. The negative aspects are the therapy bills! Modern life, perhaps more than at any other time in history, is characterized by insecurity and anxiety. We have more self-doubt and anxiety than ever before.

Shakespeare's Hamlet was advised: "Know thyself, and to thine own self be true," which echoed the maxim of the ancient Greek oracle of Delphi: "Know thyself." But today this rings hollow because modern people have no idea who they are. People sense that something seems to be missing; something more seems promised. They wonder if they aren't here to participate in something deeper and more meaningful.

That is why the biblical answers to the issues of identity and purpose are so deeply relevant to our modern life. The Bible says that our *being* (discovering our true identity) and our *becoming* (the purpose of our lives) are ultimately only found in relationship with God. So Jesus prayed: "Now this is eternal life: that they know you, the only true God, and Jesus Christ, whom you have sent" (John 17 v 3).

Genesis 1 and 2 tell us that human beings were created by God, for God, and made in his image. Entire books have been written on what it means to carry a recognizable imprint of God's nature! But let's look briefly at three aspects of our God-image that will help us understand who we are and why we are here.

We Are Spiritual

In Genesis 1 v 27-28 God creates mankind, blesses them and speaks directly to them—something he doesn't do for any of the other creatures he has made. In Genesis 2, we see Adam and Eve are able to relate to God freely in love, trust and obedience. Human beings were created to be in relationship with God. It is in relationship with God that we discover our true identity—because God alone knows the beautiful, original, unique person that he created us to be.

We Are Social

In Genesis 2, God made Adam a companion who was suitable for him. This means that we also find our true identity when we radiate God's image in our relationships with others. We have been created for self-giving and self-receiving love—to know and be known by others. Why? Because we have been made in the image of the God who exists as a loving, united community of three Persons in one: Father, Son and Holy Spirit.

We Are Stewards

Genesis 1 v 28 focuses on the task God gives to human beings to rule over his creation as his stewards, under God's gracious rule. In Genesis 2 v 19-20 Adam is given the task of naming the animals: in other words to categorize, name and define things that God has made. We are to use our God-given gifts to represent in a tangible, visible way the invisible God to the world. Our purpose, in whatever work we are called to, is to be the agents of God's rule, and reflect his creativity and beauty and order in his world.

Genesis 1 and 2 describes life before the fall (human rebellion against God). While human rebellion, as recorded in Genesis 3, damaged our God-image, it didn't destroy it altogether. That is why we see nostalgia in people who yearn for something they can't quite identify. Mark Twain wrote: "You don't quite know what it is you DO want, but it just fairly makes your heart ache, you want it so!"

When we understand God's original purpose in creating us, it helps us to live from our true center—in the way God always intended us to live.

I have an agnostic friend who is successful professionally, but not in romantic love. After a difficult break-up she told me: "Our relationship failed because I asked too much of it. I thought his love would give me a sense of identity and purpose. But he told me he couldn't bear the weight of it. Becky, why do I carry this hunger for a secure identity and for love when it can never be met? My desires mock me."

I responded: "What if your desire for identity and love are not the problem? What if that desire is not there to mock you, but to point you to something beyond yourself and beyond what anyone else can provide? Human love is wonderful, but it's not enough. Jesus tells us we have been created for God. It's in having a relationship with God through Christ that we finally discover who we are and we begin to experience the love we have been looking for."

It is in being in relationship with the true God and living as his image-bearing creatures that we are able to truly be ourselves and to find our purpose. Not only that, but understanding God's original pattern in creating us will help us to link up with the fundamental drives of every human heart. It is only as we see ourselves and see the world in this way—only as we understand our identity as God-given and God-defined, and our purpose as God-given and God-defined—that we'll truly know ourselves, and see how we can know the security and satisfaction that we were made by our Creator to enjoy.

3. The Mess We Made Of Things

Genesis 3 v 1-13, 20-24

Last week we saw that human beings were created by a good God and made in his likeness. Adam and Eve were created to love God and to live in harmony with him and the rest of creation. In love, God also gave them freedom; the freedom to choose to obey God and to reflect his ways.

People often ask why there is suffering and evil in the world if God loves his creation? Clearly something has gone terribly wrong on our planet, with world wars, genocides, terrorism, human trafficking, exploitation of children, addictions—and our personal battles with anger, pride and lust. The list goes on.

Before we look at our passage, we need to ask: *how are we to interpret this story in Genesis?* The Bible is comprised of several types of literary genre: historical and poetic among others. Determining the kind of literary style of Genesis 1 – 3 isn't easy. Is Genesis 3 a myth (stating real truths but through symbols only) or is it to be taken literally? But if it is literal, then what do we do with a story about talking snakes or fruit that seems to have magical power?

But as we look at other parts of the Bible it assumes that what we call "the fall"—the story of Genesis 3—was a real event. Just as Jesus was a real human being, whose death achieved a real salvation, so Adam was a real human being, whose sin resulted in breaking God's covenant: "Since death came through a man, the resurrection of the dead comes also through a man" (1 Corinthians 15 v 21). For what it's worth, I believe this account in Genesis 3 describes a real event, but I think the author also employs symbolism to make his point.

The important thing to recognize is what the Bible makes clear: human beings rebelled against God and his original plan, and their rebellion started the mess we see around us and in us. The Bible traces the problem back to the events of Genesis 3. The story of Adam and Eve reveals not only the marvel of creation but also what went so desperately wrong. Let's see where the problem began and what caused it.

Historical Context

God gave Adam and Eve everything they needed to flourish: a loving and intimate relationship with him and with each other, work to do and food to eat. God's plan was for them to develop and expand the garden by populating and tilling it. They were to work with God in joyful co-operation. They could meet daily with God to talk things over and ask for advice (see Genesis 3 v 8).

All of Eden was given to them with only one restriction: "You must not eat from the tree of the knowledge of good and evil, for when you eat from it you will certainly die." God placed the tree of the knowledge of good and evil in the center of the garden; it signified the importance of creatures choosing to obey their loving Creator and living in agreement with God's will. But God stated clearly what the consequences would be if they chose self-will, choosing their own knowledge and values in defiance of God. Even Eden had boundaries; they were to protect Adam and Eve by reminding them of the limits of their humanity.

God also placed the tree of life in the center of the garden. Adam and Eve were free to eat the fruit of that tree (and presumably from other trees as well). Eating the fruit from the tree of life was the sign that God had created Adam and Eve to live eternally in his presence.

 Bible Study

Read Genesis 3 v 1-7

Though the passage does not state directly who the snake is or where he comes from, the New Testament identifies him as Satan (Revelation 12 v 9; 20 v 2). Satan is not eternal like God—he is a created, rebellious angel. And he is not all-powerful like God—he does have power, but cannot defeat God or defy his purposes. Genesis 3 does not answer many of our questions about him—for instance, it does not explain why he was present in the world at that point. The writer doesn't want to answer all our queries—he wants us to focus on humanity's response to Satan and to God, and on what God does next.

1. God exercised his authority and rule in the garden through his word. How did the snake's question illustrate his craftiness and deceit (see 2 v 16-17)?

_____

_____

o Martin Luther, the 16th-century Reformer, said he found it almost impossible to translate the snake's question either into Latin or German, because, while the snake tried to sound pious, he was actually mocking God and feigning incredulity that God would even suggest such a thing—which of course God had not!

What is the serpent subtly insinuating about God's character?

_____

_____

_____

2. How does Eve's response indicate that his seduction strategy is beginning to work?

_____

_____

3. In a flat contradiction of God's word, what statements does the tempter make about the motivation of God, and the results of God's command (v 4-5)?

_____

_____

_____

o Why is it ridiculous to insinuate that God doesn't want Eve's true good, and wants to keep her on a short leash?

_____

_____

_____

4. The presence of "the tree of the knowledge of good and evil" with its prohibition reminds Adam and Eve that they are not equal to God, but must obey God. What are some reasons why taking the fruit represented such blatant defiance?

_____

_____

_____

Adam and Eve weren't merely desiring to know the difference between good and evil; they could trust God to tell them that. Rather, it was their attempt to try to live independently from God that was so serious. They wanted to decide for themselves what was right and wrong, and to set for themselves the standards by which they would live.

5. Trace the stages of Eve's downfall as she listens to the snake and chooses to misuse her freedom by disobeying God:

o She saw: What causes us to abuse the good things in God's creation (1 John 2 v 16)?

_____

_____

o She took: Why does God hold us responsible for our sin (James 1 v 13-15)?

_____

_____

o She gave: Why do you think sin likes an accomplice?

_____

_____

6. The tempter spoke half-truths that covered his basic deception (v 5). How did his statements prove partially true, but with very different results than Eve expected (v 7)?

_____

_____

7. Describe how Adam and Eve's disobedience turned God's created order upside down.

_____

_____

Read Genesis 3 v 8-24: The Shame And The Sentence

8. What is the evidence that God did not leave them in their lost condition?

_____

_____

o Why do you think God first approached them, after they sinned, by asking questions?

_____

_____

9. What immediate impact did Adam and Eve's sin have on their relationship with God and with each other (v 10-13)?

_____

_____

o List all the ways in which they justify their actions.

_____

_____

_____

10. Adam and Eve turned away from God in rebellion and he turned away from them in righteous judgment, just as he said he would. What was the outcome...

o for the snake (v 14-15)?

_____

_____

o for the woman (v 16)?

_____

_____

o for the man (v 17-19)?

_____

_____

o How do we see these judgments evident in the world around us today?

_____

_____

_____

Upon careful observation, we realize that God's judgment fits the crime. Because Eve ignored her relationship to God and Adam and acted as an independent operator, now relationships would become fraught with difficulty for her. Because Adam disobeyed God and forsook his God-given responsibilities, now the earth would not easily yield itself to him. His loving relationship to Eve was also impacted negatively.

11. What are some ways in which God demonstrated compassion for Adam and Eve (v 21)?

_____

_____

_____

God banished Adam and Eve from the garden and put the angel with the flaming sword at the gate of Eden so they couldn't return. Adam and Eve had already proved that they wanted more than the Lord had allowed them. Though God granted them a temporary reprieve, death would now be a certainty. Though not immediately obvious to us, this was God's second act of mercy...

12. Remember that eating from the tree of life signified that Adam and Eve were intended to live forever. If God allowed them to remain in the garden, eating from the fruit of the tree of life, and therefore living eternally in their ruined state, why would this actually be a cruelty and not a mercy (v 22, see also v 7-8)?

_____

_____

_____

 Live What You Learn: The Savior

Adam and Eve rejected God's rule and the perfection God had established has now been broken and destroyed by sin. Adam and Eve chose to be self-ruled. We ourselves have done the very same: "For all have sinned and fall short of the glory of God" (Romans 3 v 23). Yet God is merciful and offers hope for our human predicament.

In Genesis 3 v 15 God promises to set things right. He declares war upon the tempter. Eventually the offspring of the woman (Mary giving birth to Jesus) would crush the snake's (Satan's) head. God will not allow the snake's plan to harm his plan. This is the first promise of the gospel! Before humans rebelled, God already had in mind that there would be a Redeemer, the second Adam, Christ Jesus, who would endure suffering but bring us back to God (Ephesians 3 v 11).

o *How would you describe what is at the heart of sin?*

o *Why does doubting God's goodness and love make us vulnerable to sin?*

 ## Following Jesus: How Sin Makes Sense Of The Universe

o Modern people scoff at the notion of sin. But sin makes sense of the world we see around us and the heart we see within each of us.

o In the garden, the Serpent's strategy was to undermine Eve's confidence in God's goodness and love. He suggested that the only real value in being alive was to be God. But to be human, and dependent upon God, is wonderful, not worthless.

o Adam and Eve's disobedience reveals two things that are now characteristic of all humans:

1. Sin is the prideful claim to be in charge and call the shots.

2. Sin is the deliberate refusal to trust God and his goodness.

o *Does sin make sense of the universe?* Genesis 1 – 3 accounts for the reality of both beauty and brokenness on our planet. The problem is not metaphysical (a problem with God), but moral—we have rebelled.

o Human rebellion isn't the end of the story! The gospel enables followers of Jesus to be people of hope and not despair.

 ## Praying Together

o Is there anything in your life that is presently hindering you from developing a closer relationship with the Lord? Why not pray about it and ask for God's help.

o Thank God for all he has done to solve our problem of sin! Thank him for the great relief of not having to pretend.

o Ask God to help you not use the same excuses that Adam and Eve did when they sinned!

You'll find some more books about the themes of this session on page 61.

 # Going Deeper: Jesus' Temptation

Since the time when the first humans were tempted, the rest of humanity has been tempted as well.

We know what it is to be tempted, and what it is to give in to temptation. Jesus, while God, was also fully human. So he too was tempted; but wonderfully, he did not give in to temptation. In looking at this period where he faced great temptation, we will both marvel at his perfection and willingness to resist temptation, and we'll learn from his example. His example reminds us that being tempted to sin is not sin. Giving in to temptation is.

At Jesus' baptism, heaven was opened, the Holy Spirit descended on him in bodily form, and he heard God the Father declare: "You are my Son, whom I love; with you I am well pleased" (Luke 3 v 22).

It would have been an extraordinary experience; but then immediately, Jesus "was led by the Spirit into the wilderness, where for forty days he was tempted by the devil. He ate nothing during those days, and at the end of them he was hungry" (Luke 4 v 1-2).

The First Temptation

In the first temptation that Luke records, the devil told Jesus: "If you are the son of God, tell this stone to become bread" (v 3). The tempter used the same tactic he had used with Eve by encouraging Jesus to doubt God's word: *If* you are the Son of God... If? But God had just told Jesus he was!

The devil then tempts Jesus with food, just as he had with Eve. But what is behind this temptation? What is the devil really suggesting? *Listen Jesus, if you are really the divine Son of God, then just snap your fingers and turn stone into bread. You don't ever have to be hungry again. These pathetic, finite human creatures may have to go hungry in the desert, but not you! Just do a divine miracle!*

The fact that the enemy comes at a very vulnerable time for Jesus is significant: *Your Father isn't really looking out for your needs, Jesus, is he? Am I the only one who is concerned that you are famished? You need to take care of yourself!*

Look at the similarities between the lies told to Jesus and to Eve: that God's word can't be trusted; that God is not loving and does not want our best; that we are being deprived and must take matters into our own hands; that being human is worthless because the only thing that matters is being God.

The great deception is that Satan is asking Jesus to prove his divine identity in ways that would make Jesus demonstrate a lack of faith in God's goodness and provision.

The tempter came to Eve when she was not hungry. He came to Jesus when he was famished. Eve was surrounded by a lush garden with every provision for need at her fingertips. Jesus was in a desert and hadn't eaten in forty days. But unlike Eve, Jesus doesn't engage in conversation by dialoguing with darkness. Nor does he listen to his feelings or his stomach. Instead he says: "It is written: 'Man shall not live on bread alone'" (v 4).

God's word was Jesus' ultimate authority, just as it must be for us. Furthermore, by saying: "Man shall not live...", Jesus identifies himself with human beings, with mankind. He is not skipping over the temptation by using his divine status. He faces and endures the temptation in his humanity. He is saying: *As important as food is, our well-being is found in living in the awareness of God's promise and care. I am going to rely on him, even when he leads me into the wilderness.*

The first Adam failed and set the whole earth on the wrong track because he tried to be something he wasn't—God. But Jesus, the new, second Adam, rejects the temptation and offers us a new start because he obeyed God.

The Second Temptation

Next, Jesus is given some kind of visionary experience of the kingdoms of the earth, and Satan offers Jesus total authority with just one condition: "If you worship me, it will all be yours" (v 7). Satan offers Jesus universal power for the price of false worship.

However, even though Satan is powerful, he cannot offer Jesus everything as he claims. Whether this is merely a result of trickery or Satan's own self–delusion, he is trying to lure Jesus to grab power—but to do so Jesus must renounce God. Jesus replies by quoting Deuteronomy 6 v 13: "Worship the Lord your God and serve him only."

The first temptation tested Jesus' faith in whether God was the Provider of life's necessities. The second temptation tests whether God is the only righteous Ruler of the universe and therefore alone must be worshipped. Satan's argument is: *Come on Jesus, think of all the good you could accomplish if you had instant fame! I can give you worldwide success. You don't have to walk such a hard journey to accomplish your goals. Just compromise a little and recognize that I am the ruler of this sorry planet.*

What was Satan trying to do? Why did he want Jesus to accept his offer of power and total authority in an instant? Probably to keep Jesus from going to the cross. He was offering Jesus a shortcut—a way to glory without the suffering. But again, Jesus does what all humans are required to do: he worships God, and no one and nothing else. No shortcuts; only obedience.

The Third Temptation

Now the devil tries a clever angle and backs up his final argument with Scripture. He leads Jesus, again probably by vision, to the highest point of the temple. This temptation is exceedingly subtle: "If you are the Son of God ... throw yourself down from here," and he backs up his statement by quoting a Scripture that says the angels will protect him (Luke 4 v 9-11).

What is the enemy's strategy this time? *OK, if you insist on going through with this, then why not reveal your divinity and jump off the temple! The angels will rush to bear you up and you will wow Jerusalem! Everyone will rush to hear your wonderful message! So if you are the Son of God, then ACT like the Son of God!*

In C.S. Lewis's book, *The Screwtape Letters*, the Senior Devil, Screwtape, coaches his demonic minion on earth, Wormwood, in how to tempt "the little vermin" (as he calls humans). At one point he says to Wormwood: "You may have wondered why the Enemy [God] refuses to use his two most powerful weapons: the irresistible and the indisputable." This is precisely what Satan is trying to get Jesus to do: *just dazzle and manipulate the humans!*

What is the deception? First, jumping off the temple would not lead people to have faith in Jesus—they would simply be manipulated by the dramatic showmanship. Jesus' miracles always had a point—to point to his identity as the Servant-King, and display his kingdom. But this would be a miracle for the sole purpose of dazzling.

This temptation doesn't ask Jesus to trust God, but to tempt him. God's faithfulness doesn't need theatrics to prove his existence. God doesn't need to prove his faithfulness to us—rather, we must behave in ways that are faithful to God!

What have we learned through these temptation accounts—the first in the garden, the second in the desert? First, the enemy will always try to tempt us to doubt God's goodness and love. Once we believe that God is not good—that he cannot be trusted to take care of us—everything is poisoned. Faith is destroyed by mistrust. Once the seed of mistrust falls on receptive soil, it is only a small step before we doubt God's existence.

Second, Satan wants us to despise our humanity—to hate the fact that we have been created to depend upon God. But acknowledging our "smallness" isn't an embarrassment—it's what sets us free! It is what Jesus demonstrated by fully taking on our human nature. We have been created to depend upon a wonderful, loving God, who has only our best interests at heart. The first qualification to being used by God and becoming all that God desires us to be is acknowledging and celebrating our inadequacy! Being creatures isn't "rubbish", as Satan wants us to believe. Being creatures that depend upon God without shame, and who love and obey him, is glorious. Jesus' perfect faithfulness meant he could go to the cross to secure our forgiveness. His commitment to obeying God's word in Scripture shows us how we can resist temptation. And his love for us means that we will want to.

4. Christ The Lord Of All

Colossians 1 v 9-23

How many times have we heard someone say: "Your belief in Jesus is fine for you, but I don't buy it. I think we're all trying to get to the same place. And all roads lead to God anyway. Just don't be a fanatic by saying Jesus is the only way; or that some beliefs are true and others are false."

We are about to read a passage where the young believers in Colossae were hearing similar things: "OK, worship Jesus. Just not exclusively. Jesus is just one spirit among many to be worshiped."

So Paul writes to the Colossians an adamant declaration of Christ's supremacy over everything! Paul knew that if they weren't clear about who Christ really is, they wouldn't be strong enough to stand against these attacks.

Let's review what we have learned thus far: In our previous studies we saw that God created us to live in love, peace and harmony with him at the center. But God's perfect creation was spoilt when human beings rebelled against him—wanting to be God rather than to love and obey God.

The consequence of human rebellion was disastrous: the perfect trust and warm intimate friendship that Adam and Eve had enjoyed with God, and with each other, was destroyed. Human sin was met with God's judgment. Yet, despite their sin, God showed them great mercy because he still loved them. Though he banished them from the garden, God tenderly made clothes to better protect them than those they had constructed for themselves. Adam and Eve continued to live physically for a matter of time. But spiritually they experienced a separation from God that they had never known before. The early chapters of Genesis began with great promise and glory, but were quickly followed by the sorrow of human sin and God's judgment.

Adam and Eve set the human race on the wrong course, but we also have tried to live as if we ruled the world, instead of gladly accepting God's loving reign. The sad truth is that the entire human race needs to be reconciled to God. But how can so great a problem be solved? The chasm between God and mankind is impossible to restore by human effort. It is something only God can do, and it is something that God did.

The good news of the gospel is that sin and judgment were not the end of the story! God was not defeated by the fall. God had a plan—which he had had for all eternity—for how to rescue the planet that had turned from him.

Though God owed us nothing, in his mercy and grace he sent Christ, his Son, from heaven on a rescue mission, in order to form a people for himself and to restore everything under Christ: "to bring unity to all things in heaven and on earth under Christ" (Ephesians 1 v 10). That is what we will also discover in this marvelous passage from Colossians!

Colossians chapter 1 is one of the most majestic and profound passages in the New Testament, concerning the identity of Christ. Here we have a letter from Paul, who is so excited by his topic that his thoughts gush forth, overwhelming punctuation, sentence structure and probably the poor scribe who was writing it all down! This chapter is a burst of praise from start to finish, and it all revolves around the magnificent person of Christ Jesus. Why are we willing to surrender our entire lives to Christ Jesus? Because he is the Lord of the universe!

 ## Historical Context

Paul is under house arrest in Rome. Probably, his living conditions are not harsh, but Paul is in chains nonetheless. A visitor named Epaphras, who had most likely been converted through hearing Paul preach in Ephesus, has come to see him. Paul discovers that Epaphras has started a church in Colossae, a place where Paul has never been! But Paul learns that there is trouble. There are some who are trying to delude this young church with false teaching, which Paul fears will lead them away from the truth of the gospel—and Christ's true identity. So he calls a scribe and dictates one of his shortest but most powerful and exciting letters to this very young church in a small insignificant market town in what is modern Turkey today.

At the beginning of chapter 1 Paul examines Christ's pre-eminent role in creation, and the riches and wisdom we receive because of what he has done for us. Starting in verse 15, Paul emphasizes the Lord's work as Redeemer. To do this, Paul examines the supremacy of Christ himself.

 ## Bible Study

Read Colossians 1 v 15-23

It is commonly thought that the first section of this passage might have been a hymn or poem that celebrates who Christ is and all that he does.

1. For us today an "image" is either a copy of the original or a representation. But in the New Testament "image" is not an imitation of reality, but rather, it shares the very essence of what it is reflecting.

   Why is Jesus able to perfectly reflect God's essence in who he is, and what he does and says (v 1)?

   _____

   _____

   o What difference does it make to know that the God of Genesis 1 and 2, who is now invisible to us because of sin, has sent to us his perfect image-bearing Son in human form?

   _____

   _____

   _____

   _____

2. In verse 15 the word "firstborn" is a Jewish title that refers to Christ's honour and supremacy over all things. It doesn't mean that the Father created his Son. Even in Genesis we saw that the Trinity was involved in the act of creation. When nothing at all existed except God, God's Son already was!

List all the many ways that Jesus is supreme from verses 15-18, starting with "Christ is...".

_____

_____

_____

_____

3. What do we learn about Christ's role in the created universe (v 16)?

_____

_____

4. When Paul says in verse 17: "and in him all things hold together," it reflects what we read in Hebrews 1 v 3, where the Son is said to sustain the universe by his word of power. He is the power that keeps the entire universe in check! If Christ removed his gracious hand, we would perish in a nanosecond.

How does knowing this motivate us to worship and love Jesus?

_____

_____

_____

5. In verses 17 and 18 we are told that Christ is supreme over all powers in heaven and on earth—over all things and in all ages (see also Ephesians 1 v 22; Colossians 2 v 10). Paul also reminds us that Christ has a unique closeness to the church.

What does it mean that Christ is "the head of the body, the church" (v 18)?

_____

_____

_____

o What does this tell us concerning his love for the church and its importance?

_____

_____

Every verse Paul writes is so packed with meaning that we might miss his
reference to Christ's resurrection: He is "the firstborn from among the dead,
so that in everything he might have the supremacy" (v 18). Christ is the head
of a new restored humanity, the King for a new kingdom. Our resurrection as
new believers issues from his original and definitive resurrection; our life is
now the outflow of his risen life in us.

6. Verse 20 is the triumphant high point of this hymn: complete reconciliation. Reconciliation in the New Testament is always God's work. He, the
offended, initiates the work of reconciliation to us, the offenders. We desperately need reconciliation to God, and our earth needs renewal.

Why was reconciliation to God necessary (v 21)?

_____

_____

_____

7. What action was God, through Jesus, willing to take in order to bring us
back into a relationship with himself (v 19-22)?

_____

_____

_____

o What does it tell us about God's character, that he sent us his only Son to
achieve this?

_____

_____

8. What is the result of receiving the righteousness of Christ, according to verse 22?

_____

_____

o How do the words "reconciled," "holy in his sight," and "without blemish and free from accusation" (v 22-23) motivate you to continue firm in your faith in Christ?

_____

_____

_____

9. What is our responsibility where faith is concerned?

_____

_____

_____

10. Describe what it means to you personally to know the sacrificial measures that Jesus has taken to solve our problem?

_____

_____

_____

o How does understanding the supremacy of Christ and God's extravagant action in saving us help us grasp why Jesus is the only way to God?

_____

_____

_____

 Live What You Learn

It is a remarkable thought that through Jesus' death the barrier of sin was removed, and so it enabled a holy God to embrace a fallen world and repair its brokenness. English author and minister Peter Lewis writes that at the cross: "the explosive meeting of sin and holiness, guilt and judgment, rejection and reconciliation took place ... The final affirmation of the great hymn of Colossians 1 is that there will be no part of God's renewed universe that will be unaffected by the cross—nowhere where Calvary [the cross] is irrelevant!"

o *How will the knowledge of the fullness of Christ's identity help you to live more obediently with Christ as the Lord of your life?*

o *How do recent choices you have made about your time or money or relationships reflect Christ's supreme place in your life?*

o *How might what Christ offers us appeal to the unspoken needs of your friends who don't know Jesus yet?*

 Following Jesus: What Kind Of God Gets Angry?

o *How can a good God be angry with sin? Why can't he loosen up a bit?!*

o In human terms, we get angry when we see someone we love damaged by the consequences of their sinful choices. True love detests what destroys the beloved.

o So if God is not angry over the inevitable damage we bring upon ourselves, others and our planet, then he isn't good and he certainly isn't loving.

o *How can a good God forgive bad people without compromising his integrity?* How can he be both just and merciful?

o When the judgment had to fall, God himself became our substitute. Christ gave his life to restore our broken relationship with God. The extraordinary fact of the gospel is that God offers us grace.

o So the real question is: *what kind of God willingly sacrifices everything so that he can be in relationship with his creation?*

↑ Praying Together

○ Thank Jesus for all he has done to make you whole and reconcile you to the Father.

○ Ask God to help you understand how to more fully make Christ your Lord in the various areas of your life: your relationships; your sexuality; your work.

○ Thank God that he is perfectly holy, just and loving. Pray for people you know who do not yet realize the seriousness of God's righteous anger at their sin. Pray that they would accept his offer of grace.

You'll find some more books about the themes of this session on page 62.

↓ Going Deeper: Jesus' Present Reign

What makes Jesus different from other religious leaders? Jesus is the only founder of a world religion who is still alive! He rose from the dead, ascended into heaven and is now seated at God the Father's right hand!

Christ Is Exalted

But what is Jesus actually doing now, between his ascension 2,000 years ago and his return one day in the future? What does it actually mean to be seated at God's right hand?

It is metaphorical language for Jesus' divine omnipotence (he is all powerful) and omnipresence (he is present to all believers everywhere and at any time through his Spirit). That is why the Lord told his disciples: "Very truly I tell you, it is for your good that I am going away." (John 16 v 7). Once in heaven, Christ's presence would no longer be limited geographically as it was on earth.

To be at God's right hand means that Christ is now exalted and reigning with his Father. He is, as Paul writes, " far above all rule and authority, power and dominion, and every name that is invoked, not only in the present age but also in the one to come. And God placed all things under his feet and appointed him to be head over everything for the church" (Ephesians 1 v 21-22).

Why Is Christ's Exaltation So Important For Us?

We have all read stories of people who, having become famous, have forgotten their friends. Now that they are "somebody," they don't want to associate with the people they once knew—especially if those people have seen them humiliated or embarrassed in their old life.

Jesus suffered the greatest shame and humiliation any human being has ever known. Does he want to forget us now that he is exalted? Hardly! He took his human body and nature with him to heaven! His physical body is now glorified (as ours will be one day), but he is as he was on earth: eternally divine and everlastingly human.

That means that even in his supreme exaltation and glory, he remains one of us and committed to us. Christ is there, in the presence of God the Father, on our behalf (Hebrews 9 v 24)! It's as if he is saying: *Here I am, Father, and I'm here on behalf of the people you gave me!* Nothing should give us a deeper sense of security in the love of the triune God than that.

Our Sympathetic High Priest In Heaven

"Therefore, since we have a great high priest who has ascended into heaven, Jesus the Son of God, let us hold firmly to the faith we profess. For we do not have a high priest who is unable to empathize with our weaknesses, but we have one who has been tempted in every way, just as we are—yet he did not sin. Let us then approach God's throne of grace with confidence, so that we may receive mercy and find grace to help us in our time of need." (Hebrews 4 v 14-16)

It is a remarkable thought that the one who rules everything, and who is our representative in the heavenly throne room, knows from first-hand experience what it means to be human! He is able to stand alongside of us in whatever difficulty we experience because he remembers what it is like to be human on earth. Author Harry Blamires puts is this way: Jesus is "a God who knows exactly what it is to eat a meal and take a walk, to have a toothache or a stomach ache, to rejoice at a wedding or to mourn at a funeral..."

Our Praying High Priest

The book of Hebrews shows us that a significant part of Christ's heavenly work is that he prays for us, on our behalf, to the Father.

In the film *Bruce Almighty*, God (played by Morgan Freeman) allows a disgruntled man who is angry with God (played by Jim Carrey) to have God's powers for a few days. He nearly goes insane the first night as he is allowed to hear all the prayer requests from around the world. In desperation, he finally says "*YES!*" to everyone. The next morning the global headline is that everyone has won the lottery, but it has created pandemonium and riots worldwide as there are more winners than prize money.

The film, while not espousing Christian faith, comically reveals that human beings aren't big enough to be God. Only God in heaven has the inexhaustible kindness, power, infinite wisdom and divine grace to know how to answer prayer!

Just as he prayed for his followers on earth (Luke 22 v 31-32), Jesus prays for us now. The only thing that has changed is his location. God the Son knows what to pray for his people; God the Spirit knows how to help us pray on earth; and God the Father knows what prayers to answer for his people. When you fail to pray for what you need, out of forgetfulness or faithlessness or self-reliance, you have still been prayed for—by the Son of God. What a thought!

How much we need Christ's prayers and the power that flows from them! No matter how much we experience life's unfairness and injustices, we know that God's Son has been where we are, and he is leading us to the place where he is. He is neither unaware nor inactive. He is still working for us, devoted to us and fulfilling his Father's purposes for us.

What is our response as we see all that Christ is doing on our behalf in heaven? The author of Hebrews tells us: "Let us hold firmly to the faith we profess … Let us then approach God's throne of grace with confidence, so that we may receive mercy and find grace to help us in our time of need" (Hebrews 4 v 14, 16).

What a remedy prayer is for persecuted, harassed and just plain weary believers! In prayer we have instant access to God through Christ. We can approach the throne of grace with confidence, not because we are in any way worthy but because our high priest is infinitely worthy! But we must keep on coming, knowing that we speak to the Lord, who is in charge, who rules for and speaks to his Father on behalf of his church, who knows what we face and how we feel, and who with the Father and the Spirit is working out his purposes until the day "when the times reach their fulfillment" and God brings "unity to all things in heaven and on earth under Christ" (Ephesians 1 v 10).

5. Christ's Return

Revelation 21 v 1-8, 22-27

In our studies we've been looking at core doctrine: God's nature, his purpose in creating us, the Fall, redemption through Christ, and now Christ's return at the end of human history.

The late David Flusser, an orthodox Jewish scholar and a renowned authority on the New Testament, particularly the Gospels and early Christianity, was once asked: "As a faithful Jew you believe Messiah is coming. But if Messiah should come in your lifetime, what question would you ask him?" To which Professor Flusser replied: "Oh, that's easy. I would ask Messiah: 'Is this your first visit or your second?'"

The Bible shouts from the rooftops that Jesus came to reconcile the world to God and that he will come again! When Christ returns, it will be his second visit, not his first! His arrival will be distinctive and decisive. All of human history is moving toward that God-appointed goal. The personal return of Jesus Christ will end human history as we know it. Christ will usher in a new and endless age, the age of the new heaven and the new earth.

We began our study by looking at Genesis, the first book of the Bible, in order to understand our beginnings. We close our study by looking at Revelation, the last book of the Bible, to understand how human history ends and to see what will happen when Jesus comes again to complete God's eternal plan for salvation.

When we first start reading the Bible, it's easy to feel overwhelmed by its size and different literary styles. Though we may not see it at first, there is a plot line throughout the Bible. All of Scripture points to Christ from their particular vantage point in history—whether anticipating Messiah's coming; or announcing his arrival; or awaiting his return. For example, John, the author of Revelation, which we will be reading today, wasn't the only biblical writer to have a vision of the new heaven and new earth. The prophet Isaiah, who wrote some 700 years prior to Christ's birth, received an oracle from God: "See, I will create new heavens and a new earth. The former things will not be remembered, nor will they come to mind" (Isaiah 65 v 17). Ezekiel, a prophet who wrote about 600 years before Christ's birth, was also allowed a glimpse into eternity in which he saw "what looked like a throne ... and high above on the throne was a figure like that of a man" (Ezekiel 1 v 26).

Our passage today in Revelation 22 brings to a close the plot-line of the entire Bible, linking everything together, with references to Genesis and Isaiah all the way through to Christ and his work of re-creation. All of which is terribly exciting, as we shall see!

 ## Historical Context

The book of Revelation is widely assumed to have been written by the apostle John while he was exiled on the island of Patmos. We cannot be certain when it was written, but the most likely date is AD 81-96. It was written for the benefit of the early Christian church that was undergoing severe persecution, so that they might not compromise their faith. While the author uses several literary styles, his main style is called "apocalyptic," which uses symbolism to convey its message. ("Apocalypse" means revelation or unveiling.)

John is given a series of visions in which God allows him to see what is going on "behind the scenes" of human history. The main text for today, Revelation 21 v 1-8, points us to what the new world to come will be like. It shows how all things—heaven and earth and the community of God's redeemed people—will be made new, or perhaps more accurately, will be renewed!

Remember that the apostle John was there at the very beginning of Christ's ministry. He was part of the core group (along with James and Peter) who were closest to Jesus and who had witnessed key events in Jesus' life, such as his transfiguration. He was at the foot of the cross when Jesus asked him to care for his mother, Mary. He was a significant leader in the early church in Jerusalem, and he was now witnessing the severe persecution of Christians.

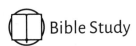 **Bible Study**

Read Revelation 21 v 1-8

1. Because of human rebellion in Genesis 3, God's presence withdrew. What remarkable event will God initiate between heaven (where God now dwells) and earth at the new creation (v 2)?

_____

_____

What an extraordinary thought, to realize that God himself will bring heaven to earth!

2. In Genesis 1 and 2 the Bible begins with a picture of the world and the loving Creator who designed it—human beings enjoying perfect harmony with the rest of the created order in a garden. But Adam and Eve became alienated from God because of their rebellion.

How is our relationship with God described in the new creation (v 3-5)?

_____

_____

_____

o How does the new creation differ from life, as we now know it, after the fall?

_____

_____

_____

3. Who is seated on the throne, and why is his word reliable (v 5-6)?

_____

_____

In the Bible God performed three extremely significant and creative acts on behalf of mankind, which are followed by three similar statements. Two have happened and one is yet to come. When God completed his work of creating the universe, we are told he rested, not out of exhaustion but because "God had finished the work he had been doing" (Genesis 2 v 2). When Jesus fulfilled his mission right up to the point of his sacrificial death, he cried from the cross: "It is finished" (John 19 v 30). Now in verse 6, John is allowed a glimpse of what the new creation will be like, and he hears Christ say from the eternal throne: "It is done!"

4. How does each event (creation, cross, new creation) build on the one before?

_____

_____

_____

o In what way is the new creation the completion of Christ's work on behalf of mankind?

_____

_____

_____

Just because Christ's work is complete doesn't mean that the redeemed will spend eternity strumming harps. When heaven comes to earth there will be a fullness of joy and perfect fellowship with God and with each other—and faithful servants will be given new tasks (Luke 19 v 11-27). The early church leader Irenaeus speculated: "God will always have something more to teach man, and man will always have something more to learn from God."

5. What does it mean to be thirsty and how is our thirst quenched (v 6)?

_____

_____

_____

6. What does it mean to be "victorious," and what are those who are "victorious" promised (v 7)?

_____

_____

_____

7. Who are the ones who will miss out on the joy and benefits of the new creation?

_____

_____

_____

As C. S. Lewis wrote: "There are only two kinds of people in the end: those who say to God, 'Thy will be done,' and those to whom God says, in the end, 'Thy will be done.' All that are in Hell, choose it. Without that self-choice there could be no Hell. No soul that seriously and constantly desires joy will ever miss it. Those who seek find. Those who knock find the door opened."

Read Revelation 21 v 22-27

8. Why is there no temple in the new creation?

_____

_____

o Why is there no need for the sun or moon?

_____

_____

In times past God symbolically dwelt with his people in the temple in Jerusalem—specifically in the Most Holy Place, where only one priest could enter just once a year. After the destruction of the temple by the Babylonians, God prophesied through Ezekiel that he would build a new temple.

That promise was fulfilled through the life, death and resurrection of Jesus (John 2 v 19-22). As Christians, we now know God's presence dwelling with us through the Holy Spirit. Our knowledge isn't perfect due to our human limitations and frailty. But we are promised that one day we shall know him fully. When Christ returns, we shall all live in the new heaven and new earth. There will be no special place in the new creation where God's presence is focused, because the entire earth will be his temple! There will never again be distance between God and us for we shall know him perfectly!

Live What You Learn

Imagine the relief that John's visions would have given those Christians suffering great persecution. His visions reminded them (and us!) that God is in control. There may be times when we don't understand what God is doing in the world but he is still in charge. While it may all seem chaotic on earth, we must remember that it is a conquered chaos. History is moving toward a conclusion. Christ will return and make all things right. Therefore our task on earth is to remain faithful while we worship and trust the living God.

o *How do these glorious truths about our future impact how we live now?*

o *Why should they galvanize us to bear witness to an unbelieving world?*

Following Jesus: How Then Do We Live?

o Human history is moving toward a God-appointed goal—Christ's return. So what are we to do as we wait? *Watch* and *work* (Matthew 25 v 13).

o *What should characterize our lives as we wait?* Through Christ, God adopts us as his children. In Romans 8 v 15-17 we are told that:

1. God gives us security (v 15)—we need not fear being rejected.

2. God gives us authority (v 17)—because the world belongs to our Father.

3. God gives us intimacy (v 15)—a relationship characterized by love.

4. God gives us assurance (v 16)—through his Spirit.

o We are also to *work* for Christ by being his witnesses (Matthew 28 v 19). *How?*

— First, listen—understand people's beliefs and their longings.

— Sensitively and lovingly share the good news of Christ.

— Work for justice in a broken world.

Praying Together

o Thank God that our hope is certain in him. Ask God to help you look at life through his promises and to remember all that he has done for you.

o Memorize this verse: "'For I know the plans I have for you,' declares the LORD, 'plans to prosper you and not to harm you, plans to give you hope and a future'" (Jeremiah 29 v 11). Thank God for this promise.

o Ask God to open your eyes to the unbelievers he is seeking and to use you in their lives.

o Ask God to show you where you can serve the poor or minister in areas of injustice.

You'll find some more books about the themes of this session on page 62.

Going Deeper: Making All Things New: The Four R's

I was talking to a skeptic one day who, after a long discussion about the evidence for faith, said: "Do you know what strikes me the most about you? You seem to be a person of hope and not despair."

Why do Christians have hope? Primarily, for two reasons: first, because God sent his Son to reconcile the world to himself; second, because one day Christ will return to make all things new.

Christ came to reconcile us to God through dying on the cross for our sin. When we come to Christ in faith and repentance, Jesus forgives our sins and makes us a new creation by giving us the Spirit, who indwells us. But Christ's coming didn't erase all of the effects of sin on our planet. Human beings still experience hardship, injustice, disease and death. It is only when Christ returns that evil will be destroyed, sin will be over, and he will make all things new.

With that in mind, let's look at the four things Christ will do when he returns:

1. There Will Be A Reckoning

The Bible says the dead from every generation past and present will be raised from death and Christ will judge all who have ever lived (see John 5 v 28-29; 3 v 18, 36). As moderns who live in an age of "selected tolerance," we struggle with how a loving God can judge sin. But the truth remains, that for those who have refused God's offer of grace, their tragic insistence to live apart from God's presence will be honored. God will not violate their will, or compromise his perfect plan for his creation. But Christians should not approach Jesus' judgment with fear. After all, the Judge we shall meet on the Day of Judgment is the Jesus we have known and loved in this life. He is the very one that has dealt with our sin, through taking it upon himself. If we have placed our trust in him, we can be secure. "There is now no condemnation for those who are in Christ Jesus" (Romans 8 v 1).

2. There Will Be A Reunion With Jesus

When Christ returns, we will see him face to face! If we die before he returns, we shall be with the Lord, just as he told the thief on the cross (Luke 23 v 42-43). But life in heaven, though utterly joyous, is temporary. It is only at Christ's return that we will witness the full culmination of human history. As part of the apostle John's vision of future eternity, Revelation 21 v 3 proclaims: "God's dwelling place is now among the people, and he will dwell with them. They will be his people, and God himself will be with them and be their God." That means we can live our present lives with courage and joy because we know the end that awaits us. Whether we die before Christ returns, or he returns in our lifetime, one thing is certain: we shall be with our Lord! Our hope is certain, for one day faith will become sight and hope will be fulfilled, and our whole being will be united with the God we love. All that we have longed for will be ours and we will be his.

3. There Will Be A Resurrection For All Believers

At Christ's return we will receive our resurrected bodies, just as Jesus did at his resurrection. What will our new bodies be like? We do not know everything about them, but we do know that they will be like Jesus' resurrected body, which was physical but not subject to all the limitations of our natural bodies.

His resurrection was a "preview of coming attractions" for us! The Bible tells us that in our bodies we will enjoy feasting with the Lord Jesus, enjoying a world where loved ones no longer die, and where there are no more tears or sorrow or anything to hurt us anymore. It is this wonderful hope that sustains us in times of difficulty and suffering. No aches or pains or disabilities; just the supreme blessing of being with the Lord Jesus (see 1 Corinthians 15 v 52-54; 1 Thessalonians 4 v 16-17 and Hebrews 11 v 35).

4. There Will Be Renewal

When the Bible speaks of Christ making a new heaven and new earth, it's not speaking of an alternative to this world; it is speaking of the healing and restoration of this world!

Jesus will renew the whole earth and heaven. But this time heaven will come to us! There is a uniting of heaven and earth so that they will no longer be separated as they are now, but will be one. Romans 8 v 18-25 tells us that when Christ returns, "the creation itself will be liberated from its bondage to decay and brought into the freedom and glory of the children of God." When Jesus returns, we will find ourselves in our present, but renewed, bodies, in a renewed earth and heaven.

Evil doesn't have the last word—God does. Satan shall be led to his doom. And there will be no more separation or illness or grief. God's people will be united to God and to each other, for the old will have gone and the new will be here. This is truly a future worth getting excited about!

Peter Lewis writes in *The Glory of Christ*: "Yet our hope is not really the city with its perfect architecture and untarnished building materials. They are as asphalt compared to the real glory of that city. For our hope is not merely the place, nor even the privilege of participating in the gathering of the rescued people; our hope is the Person himself in whose presence we will know the fullness of joy— we will be forever with the Lord! The hope God gives has always gone beyond the where, to the who. God, who has called us into fellowship with his Son Jesus Christ our Lord, is faithful."

That means we live our lives praying for Christ's return and at the same time working for God's glory as we prepare to see him one day face to face! That is why the choices we make now are so important, for they define us and shape our future existence, not only in terms of where we spend eternity, but also in terms of the person we are becoming. This is why the conversations we have are so important, for we can show and share the invitation Jesus extends to all people to enjoy his new creation for ever. This is why we have hope, no matter how hard life may become. As Tim Keller puts it:

"We know that we are not what we will one day be, that we do not already have all that we one day will have. We know that all our best days lie ahead of us, and that one day all our painful days will lie behind us. We wait eagerly, and yet also patiently." (*Romans 8-16 For You*)

And we join with the apostle John in the penultimate verse of the Bible by saying:

"Come, Lord Jesus" (Revelation 22 v 20).

Useful Resources

Books on doctrine and the story of the Bible:

Bible Doctrine (Wayne Grudem)

Concise Theology (J.I. Packer)

Know the Truth (Bruce Milne)

At the Heart of the Universe (Peter Jensen)

God's Big Picture (Bible overview) (Vaughan Roberts)

Session One: The Beginning

The First Chapters of Everything (Alasdair Paine)

Delighting in the Trinity (UK title: *The Good God*) (Michael Reeves)

Is God Really in Control? (Jerry Bridges)

Work Matters (Tom Nelson)

Session Two: How Life Was Meant To Be

What Makes us Human? (Mark Meynell)

Knowing God (J.I. Packer)

Big God (Orlando Saer)

Session Three: The Mess We Made Of Things

Why Suffering? (Ravi Zacharias & Vince Vitale)

Counterfeit Gods (Timothy Keller)

Unspeakable (Os Guinness)

The Envy of Eve (Melissa Kruger)

Did the Devil Make Me Do It? (Mike McKinley)

Session Four: Christ The Lord Of All

The Incomparable Christ (John Stott)

The Resurrection in your Life (Mike McKinley)

The Glory of Christ (Peter Lewis)

Is Forgiveness Really Free? (Michael Jensen)

Session Five: Christ's Return

Heaven (Randy Alcorn)

Last Things First (Graham Beynon)

How Will the World End? (Jeramie Rinne)

Eternity Changes Everything (Stephen Witmer)

LIVE | GROW | KNOW

Also available in the range:

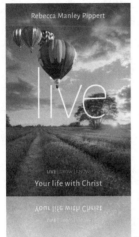

Live

In this first part of her series exploring the Christian life, Becky looks at what the gospel is and how we know it's true, what the Christian life is like, and how to start and keep going as a follower of Christ—how to really LIVE. Ideal for new Christians and not-yet-Christians as well as more long-standing believers. *With accompanying DVD and online downloads.*

Grow

In the second instalment of the LiveGrowKnow series, Becky looks at how we grow as Christians. God wants us to do more than just keep going in faith—he wants us to be growing in our faith, love and joy. And, as Becky explains, he has given us various ways to GROW. *With accompanying DVD and online downloads.*

For more information, visit:
thegoodbook.com/livegrowknow
the goodbook.co.uk/livegrowknow

thegoodbook
COMPANY
Opening up the Bible

At The Good Book Company, we are dedicated to helping Christians and local churches grow. We believe that God's growth process always starts with hearing clearly what he has said to us through his timeless word—the Bible.

Ever since we opened our doors in 1991, we have been striving to produce resources that honor God in the way the Bible is used. We have grown to become an international provider of user-friendly resources to the Christian community, with believers of all backgrounds and denominations using our Bible studies, books, evangelistic resources, DVD-based courses and training events.

We want to equip ordinary Christians to live for Christ day by day, and churches to grow in their knowledge of God, their love for one another, and the effectiveness of their outreach.

Call us for a discussion of your needs or visit one of our local websites for more information on the resources and services we provide.

North America: www.thegoodbook.com
UK & Europe: www.thegoodbook.co.uk
Australia: www.thegoodbook.com.au
New Zealand: www.thegoodbook.co.nz

North America: 866 244 2165
UK & Europe: 0333 123 0880
Australia: (02) 6100 4211
New Zealand (+64) 3 343 2463

www.christianityexplored.org

Our partner site is a great place for those exploring the Christian faith, with a clear explanation of the good news, powerful testimonies and answers to difficult questions.

One life. What's it all about?